Be Still:

Poems for Kay Sage

Be Still:

Poems for Kay Sage

by

Nadia Arioli

© 2023 Nadia Arioli. All rights reserved.
This material may not be reproduced in any form, published,
reprinted, recorded, performed, broadcast,
rewritten or redistributed without
the explicit permission of Nadia Arioli.
All such actions are strictly prohibited by law.

Cover image by Nadia Arioli
Cover design by Shay Culligan
Author photo by Nadia Arioli

ISBN: 978-1-63980-404-7

Kelsay Books
502 South 1040 East, A-119
American Fork, Utah 84003
Kelsaybooks.com

*Dieses Baums Blatt, der von Osten
Meinem Garten anvertraut,
Giebt geheimen Sinn zu kosten,
Wies den Wissenden erbaut,*

*Ist es Ein lebendig Wesen,
Das sich in sich selbst getrennt?
Sind es zwei, die sich erlesen,
Daß man sie als Eines kennt?*

*Solche Frage zu erwidern,
Fand ich wohl den rechten Sinn,
Fühlst du nicht an meinen Liedern,
Daß ich Eins und doppelt bin?*

—Goethe, *Gingo Bilboba*

Acknowledgments

Grateful acknowledgement is given to the editors of the following publications, where versions of these poems previously appeared:

As It Ought To Be: "I Walk Without Echo" (nominated for Best of the Net in 2021), "The Fourteen Daggers," "A Bird in the Room," "The Answer Is 'No'"

Black Coffee Review: "Tomorrow, Mr. Silber"

Blue as an Orange: "This Silent World," "Tomorrow Is Never," "Le Passage," "Suspension Bridge for the Sparrows"

The Blue Nib: "The Upper Side of the Sky," "Small Portrait," "Be Still"

Can We Have Our Ball Back: "This Instant," "Song of Sevens" "Nests of Lightning," "Reflex Arc," "Unusual Thursday"

Cider Press Review: "The Giants Dance"

Coffin Bell: "Monolith," "A Little Later"

Flight of the Dragonflies Journal: "In the Third Sleep," "Festa," "Ring of Iron, Ring of Wool"

Former People: A Journal of Bangs, Whimpers, Arts, Culture, and Commentary: "My Room has Two Doors," "I Saw Three Cities"

Gasher: "Near the Five Corners"

Gyroscope: "All Surroundings Are Referred to High Water"

Heavy Feather Review: "Starlings, Caravans"

Lime Hawk: "Dreamy Cars for Waterbury"

Penn Review: "Handle with Care"

SoftBlow: "The Outline of Silence"

SWWIM Every Day: "Journey to Go"

Trampoline Poetry: "Pour Yves," "Listen to the Wind"

Voicemail Poems: "Bounded on the West by the Land Under Water" (nominated for Best of the Net 2021)

West Trestle Review: "On The First of March, Crows Begin to Search" (nominated for Best of the Net 2021)

Whale Road Review: "Day Without Name"

What Are Birds? Literary Journal: "A Finger on the Drum," "At the Appointed Time"

Writer's Garret Presents Turn a Phrase: "Unicorns Came Down to the Sea," "Point of Intersection"

Contents

I.

On "Monolith" by Kay Sage   15
On "A Little Later" by Kay Sage   16
On "My Room Has Two Doors" by Kay Sage   17
On "I Walk Without Echo" by Kay Sage   18
On "Danger, Construction Ahead" by Kay Sage   20
On "Pour Yves" by Kay Sage   21
On "Listen to the Wind" by Kay Sage   22
On "I Have No Shadow" by Kay Sage   23
On "A Finger on the Drum" by Kay Sage   24
On "At the Appointed Time" by Kay Sage   26
On "Margin of Silence" by Kay Sage   27
On "Chrysalis" by Kay Sage   28
On "The Fourteen Daggers" by Kay Sage   31

II.

On "Shivering Mountain" by Kay Sage   35
On "Journey to Go" by Kay Sage   38
On "Handle with Care" by Kay Sage   39
On "Near the Five Corners" by Kay Sage   40
On "The Hidden Letter" by Kay Sage   41
On "Too Soon for Thunder" by Kay Sage   43
On "The Giants Dance" by Kay Sage   44
On "Secret Voyage of a Spark" by Kay Sage   45
On "I Saw Three Cities" by Kay Sage   46
On "The Upper Side of the Sky" by Kay Sage   47
On "Midnight Street" by Kay Sage   49
On "In the Third Sleep" by Kay Sage   51
On "Bounded on the West by the Land Under
    Water" by Kay Sage   53
On "Festa" by Kay Sage   54

On "On the First of March, Crows Begin to Search" by Kay Sage	56
On "Ring of Iron, Ring of Wool" by Kay Sage	57
On "The Seven Sleepers" by Kay Sage	59
On "All Surroundings Are Referred to High Water" by Kay Sage	60
On "Mother of Time" by Kay Sage	62
On "Unicorns Came Down to the Sea" by Kay Sage	63

III.

On "Starlings, Caravans" by Kay Sage	67
On "This Is Another Day" by Kay Sage	74
On "Tomorrow, Mr. Silber" by Kay Sage	75
On "The Instant" by Kay Sage	77
On "Small Portrait" by Kay Sage	78
On "Song of Sevens" by Kay Sage	79
How to Give: On "Page 49" by Kay Sage	80
On "The Outline of Silence" by Kay Sage	82
On "Nests of Lightning" by Kay Sage	86
On "Unusual Thursday" by Kay Sage	87
On "Reflex Arc" by Kay Sage	89
On "Men Working" by Kay Sage	90
On "A Short Day" by Kay Sage	91
On "The Point of Intersection" by Kay Sage	93
On "On the Contrary" by Kay Sage	94
On "Dreamy Cars for Waterbury" by Kay Sage	95
On "Third Paragraph" by Kay Sage	96
On "No Passing" by Kay Sage	97

IV.

On "A Bird in the Room" by Kay Sage	101
On "Day Without Name" by Kay Sage	103
On "The Circle Never Sleeps" by Kay Sage	104
On "Signal to Signal" by Kay Sage	106
On "This Silent World" by Kay Sage	107
On "Tomorrow Is Never" by Kay Sage	109
On "Le Passage" by Kay Sage	110
On "Suspension Bridge for the Sparrows" by Kay Sage	111
On "South to Southwesterly Winds Tomorrow" by Kay Sage	112
On "Detour" by Kay Sage	114
On "The Answer Is No" by Kay Sage	116
On "A Change in the Water Table" by Kay Sage	117
On "Quote, Unquote" by Kay Sage	119
On "Questions Going Nowhere" by Kay Sage	122
On "No Wind, No Birds" by Kay Sage	124
On "Watching the Clock" by Kay Sage	125
Be Still: Poems for Kay Sage	126

I.

On "Monolith" by Kay Sage

This is the end of useless light.
Think of the lights that are no
more. The last fireflies of the year—
your face when you used to talk about art.
My headlights make little difference
anymore, all turns to coffee grounds
feeling, driving along the shore.
And when my cigarette blooms
between my fingers,
what gesture, what punctuation,
for no one but ghosts in the garage.
All the useless light goes here,
this monolith. It'll be in your throat
like a cough-drop, a gross glottal stop.
I learned that morticians use
spiked contacts to keep eyes
from opening. This, too, is last communion.

On "A Little Later" by Kay Sage

these are the things i keep in my pocket
ladder parts a pill two eggs
things that will take you there

i was born with eggs in my pocket
bounced around europe married
unmarried a world war broke out
and then married once more in America
loves brain burst blood vessels kneading
skull like cat a little later ladder
took the form of gun

you have keys and string in your trousers
museum ticket stubs
i have clutter of sad images i paint
them out they are not for you
but you can have them just
the same   like grabbing the wrong umbrella
after a wedding funeral or birth
the only person who can decide which is you

On "My Room Has Two Doors" by Kay Sage

The places you can go by to egg
these days. To mornings as crisp
as sheets, or back inside your mother
when you were not yet you. Cramped
compartments are expected anyways
when traveling by bus or train,
and the yolk will give you shine.

An arch, too, is equally serviceable
if you want to go. I always hold
my breath when going through that
kind of door. The weight will want
to come back, surely, from where
the builders carved it away from stone.

My room has two doors,
but when you died, it had none.
It was as if I were a light bulb
and grief a mouth. I went in
with no hope of passing.
Teeth prevented my leaving.

I have seen my birth and my death,
both are plain enough. But what
is this green light that suffuses,
and why is my life but one room?

On "I Walk Without Echo" by Kay Sage

To be a woman is to be caustic
with no power. To instigate

but not to burn. A bellyless earthquake,
a doctor's bill that goes on and on.

They say we were made second.
Helpmate, companion, never the main

story. A plot point in a chapter
about blood. We go back,

the feminine parts of ourselves,
fetus Matryoshka dolls.

My mother said I looked like one
as a baby. I thought she meant I *was*

one. I learned in an encyclopedia
I was right. My mother was in utero

with ova. An ovum became half
of me. I've still got most my eggs.

To be second but half already there
and while carrying half of the next feels

like a mathematical anomaly,
the kind that would fill a volume.

I sat holding up my dress, bent into three
points: head, knees, one between. Lips

out like shellfish. I want to walk
without echo. I wait on a porcelain ear.

I picture it—perfectly round O's
of red. Such a bright color in the dark.

I will it: I walk without echo.
Bleed, damn you.

On "Danger, Construction Ahead" by Kay Sage

You don't have to be luminous.
You don't have to chirp on
like a zealous hostess,
talking as if we were all small dogs.
The lights and trees and alcohol
will do it for you. Just stand
there and smile, if you can manage.

December is the month for squinting,
while you stand behind the punchbowl,
fists smoothing skirt. December is a city
you finally found a road out of. Take it
by night. Feed the horses first.

December for seeing the moth
and being the moth. A plate
of dessert in light. You don't have
to have color. Everyone is a moth here.

//////

I gave you a canoe one year.
You said it reminded you of a coffin,
always one for crassness.
How it grew, rowboat the size of Rome
then Europe. It terrified the onlookers,
who soon had little rowboats of their own.

December is the month for fear.
December for shouldery architecture.
December for danger. Construction ahead
in the new year. December for deciding
what sort of failures we deserve this time.

On "Pour Yves" by Kay Sage

I use my fingers to know the real
when my body strives to undo itself.

A straight road will collapse—
side touching side in the distance,
except if you were to walk and feel
the width is the same.

A tree will dance,
but if you lick your finger
and hold it out,
you'll know it's just the wind.

I've never seen floating colors,
colors that aren't attached to the back
of things. But I have color in tubes
and on pallet. Some I won't let out.

For you, Yves, a small miracle.
A thing that is and is not real.
Who are we to tell trees
they are not dancing,
roads they won't meet themselves?

I've seen snail shells in the garden,
on the undersides of plants.
You can touch them with your fingers.
You can bring them home.

On "Listen to the Wind" by Kay Sage

I am defeathered gull.
I have turned to innards,
nothing else left to examine.

I, immortal and listless,
hide under cars, cry when
it rains, go to bars mid-afternoon.

Always for me it is mid-afternoon,
waiting for a twilight that never comes.
Nothing about me isn't boil,

isn't overgrown tissue. I am
overfilling myself like wind
overfills tablecloths.

When bars fill up, I slip
out. I've been to all holes.
Without even thinking, I can find

this one again. I don't collect
my threadbare coat, don't
pay my bill. Find the hole

that is under the city. Listen
to the wind. I unfold myself
an umbrella, wait.

On "I Have No Shadow" by Kay Sage

I didn't want to learn how to dance
so much as learn how to take dancing lessons.

Never could I abide a hand
on my shoulder, a voice telling

my feet where to go.
Now, I have no shadow.

This, Mom, is an apology, of sorts.

On "A Finger on the Drum" by Kay Sage

This is the body I have always wanted.

Taut Cyprus, ponderous finger.

I have overcome trypophilia—

skin smooth shell, watertight.

No eyes, nose, ears, mouth,

I have given up being in love with a wound.

I told God: Make me stop finding

holes to nurse. Make me without a cunt.

And, look, I sprung up, dead,

genderless Aphrodite. They did not

find me beautiful, find me catching,

now that I have learned life without leaking.

I loped to the desert, past the

grasslands and deer. I the only

tree for miles, I the only empty gesture.

Below me are two hares,

they share a fearsome secret. One

puts a finger on the drum.

Most days are the same here,

the few animals make their animal lives.

A wonder I can see anything at all—

sand rising and falling,

as many spaces as grains,

clouds a horrid, porous strip.

On "At the Appointed Time" by Kay Sage

I have seen animals from both sides—
fur and meat. Down by the Mediterranean
coast, the birds and fish go to golden light,
soft and singing each to each.
Scales and feathers both are fur.

The meat side we take for granted—
that all animals have innards,
are not balloons. Look at your plate.
Pork belly, lamb shank, salmon.
Serviceable and neat, like a housewarming gift.

I have seen animals from both sides,
but never the same one. It seemed
too much to know. That was the year
I swore off the duck my father raised, even their eggs.
But you, love, I want as dissection,

as piñata, as clock I can take apart.
Let us go to a little dock
at the appointed time. Discard our clothes
over the edge in seaweed heap. Place
our hands on the obelisk and wait.

Here is where we will switch dreams.
You'll dream of feathers and ponds.
I do not know what I will dream of.
I want to see you inside and out.
It'll hurt but a little. Only in dreams

do impending things feel like peace.
I'm ready to begin.

On "Margin of Silence" by Kay Sage

I am no mammal.
Can you imagine me having blood,
let alone blood that is warm?
I have a hole where breast

should be. Motherhood
like absence I have built
my person around.
You can find me by the edge

of the sea, hairless as any
mollusk. I thought I too
were shell, but nothing
fills in my corners.

You demanded to know what
I am, having only known
a woman by the warmth
between her thighs.

I am the key that goes nowhere.
I am the lint in your pocket,
the shrieks of a maid. I am
a hand full of pills.

I keep a margin of silence
around me like shadow.
There will be no note,
at least, no note for you.

On "Chrysalis" by Kay Sage

I want to tell you about a painting I saw in a book once. There is a corridor made of elephant. One figure crouches at the opening. It is made of elephant too. At the far end is another figure, which appears to be dancing. The light is a twilight hush. The shadows grow long.

***

You had taught me about the Hero's Journey, using a big marker and a great patience. I remember the eight steps. I know that there are allies gathered earlier on, but I want to remind you that they're with you, in the belly of the beast, if that's where you are.

***

I read the painting backwards. Right to left. Perhaps this is because the crouching figure is closest to the viewer on the right, and the left figure is far away, like how the future is always murky, especially after passing through tunnels of beast. One can hope, at least, that there will be dancing.

***

A decade ago, I lugged my shitty furniture into your then-girlfriend's apartment, and you made me a sandwich. We weren't yet friends.

You always sit on the floor, like a child. It is strange to think of you in a room on a white, folding chair. But perhaps, since this is in a church, there's pews.

Four years ago, I thought I had made it from the belly of the beast into the step called Transformation. I walked 18 miles for my birthday. Despite liking painting and poetry more than moving, more than getting anything done. Despite having driven a screwdriver through the length of my left foot, starting with my heel then out the little toe and back again. Methodical and without flinching

On my birthday, I walked 18 miles. It was for suicide prevention. My mother had slit both her wrists, elbow to thumb joint. She used a knife. She didn't die but made a point of telling me this was my fault. Methodical and without flinching.

I said no. I was going to do something. And that walk felt like transformation. It took all night. You were there, you hugged me.

But the next day, I didn't believe in transformation anymore. 30 miles away, while I was walking, my other friend had passed. They say he did it in his sleep.

***

The title of the painting is *Chrysalis*. Neither side of the tunnel is lighter, just different.

***

This week, I watched a thriller. In the thriller, the hero and his girlfriend had a countdown. Four minutes to untie themselves from a nuclear missile. I paused the film and rewound it back. I was trying to give them more time.

***

I am so sorry your mother died.

***

I am not sure what else to say. It was easier when I had nothing to write about except paintings. Ekphrasis. I picked out this painting before this week even happened. I am methodical.

I am trying to learn gentleness.

When you come back, having passed through, I'll learn how to make you a vegetarian sandwich. My floor is huge. We can move aside the laundry I've been meaning to put away. I'll hug you. I won't let go.

On "The Fourteen Daggers" by Kay Sage

All the prosaic thin places you will visit
are before you. The places where reality
shifts a bit to the right like a staircase
or fourteen daggers that fail to kill you.

A movie theater in a foreign city
where you are alone. You sit in front
of the projector directly. A story bounces
around your head. A laundromat,
any time, any place. Things are getting
clean without you.

The tobacco store where the man
with thick glasses coughs a little worse
each year. A gas station with maps
of the Midwest for sale. The state-lines
look menacing. The old ship,
below deck, where buckets cluster
like drippy ulcers.

A smaller place is your mouth after
your first nosebleed. You saw what happened
to your teeth when you smiled for the mirror.
When you were a teenager, you filled your palms
with wet bees for the watery shudder.

The eighth dagger is you.
O my Angelica root,
O my toothy abortion.

I will not say what the other six are.
I can't even see the last. Perhaps
it is shaped like a gun.

If a third were to see us,
they would know which was you
and which was I.
I am the beginning, you are the middle
and more like a knife.

But perhaps we are in each other's houses
now, switched like interpreting a dream badly.
The waiting room was the thinnest place.
My breasts are scalloped like fingernails.

II.

On "Shivering Mountain" by Kay Sage

—For Jesse

1.

What is the view like in New York? I have never been, but I picture buildings as tall as your ideals, streets as crowded as your mind. I picture you in a torn coat, sleeping in a heap like some animal, like a shivering mountain. I forget it's summertime. The seasons still march on, even if you're unhoused.

You asked me for dough to get somethin' to eat.
Since we last spoke, you live on the street.
Yeah, I wouldn't believe all the shit that you've seen.

2.

I started as your friend from the porch in college. Little oddballs who liked smoking outside. Now it's like this painting by Kay Sage. Now it's like a song by St. Vincent. It doesn't matter. You hate art. But if this were back then, you would have listened to me anyways.

Once, I had front-row tickets to you getting lost inside yourself— like watching a child bury himself in bedsheets by heading the wrong way for air. I'm mixing my metaphors. What I'm trying to say is, I heard you say impossible things and tricked you into going to the hospital. What I'm trying to say is, I thought I'd never hear from you or about you again, and I wish I were right.

You bounced around, found obtuse religions and streets. And you wrote letters about your friends being rapists and murderers and about how the photographs of you were faked. You threatened to blow up a school. You could do it, too. I read what you have to say, sometimes, to make sure you're not dead.

3.

My husband and I have a song we like to sing, being ridiculous and useless people. It's a duet.

Has anybody seen my wallet?
You usually put it right there.
I'm going to put it in my pocket.
You usually put it right there.

It is a comfort to know where things are and where they go, that even if you've misplaced something, it is not irretrievably lost.

4.

Not that you are a wallet. I wouldn't put you in my pocket anyways. I am taking back-row seat this time. Even further back than that. I'm not even in the same room.

You told me our friend had raped you, freshman year. I told you I can't have this conversation with you, right now. It was not a matter of belief. I just couldn't. You told me I acted like I was better than you and said you didn't care.

When I said, "Let me think,"
and you yelled through your teeth

I want to tell you "We all love you." But I know that's not enough.

5.

This is the view from the porch. Small excuse for shelter, but I can't go near the shivering mountain. I am not in the same room, but I am as always on the porch. I am an egg, unmoving and not too different than an eye. I see you, your shape masked and twisted. You cradle part of yourself. Somewhere in there, I'm afraid you carry a gun.

When you get free, Johnny,
I hope you find peace.

On "Journey to Go" by Kay Sage

When I knew you, everything I owned was chapped.
A wooden fence around my yard,
white with brown beneath.
Do you know that ache?
The dustcovers of my books went peely.
My face did it too—
nose a terrible melon, mouth like Pompeii.

Not the crumbling but the moment before.
Like stepping on the lip of a canyon.
My insides went fluidic. If you
were to open my stomach, an ocean
would fall out. A deep-fried human
with something undercooked between skins.

But I am making the journey to smooth.
I no longer know your name.
Look how I become unfeathered.
My torso is runner's knee before the gun.
I am tooth; I will bite air.

When I knew you, I shook, unable to paint,
or smile, or stand. A polyphony of poor taste.
I thought it was nerves, but it was just
my skeleton starting to hatch.

On "Handle with Care" by Kay Sage

Beware the gentle things in the garden.
They will take you out. They
are small but have mouths.

Beware the mouths in the garden.
They are small and have insect designs.
They are gentle but take out your garden.

This is the hum of infection. Gentle mouths
singing in dissonance. Mouth garden
will take. I go to snail.

Hum a lullaby to a baby that isn't there.
I pace the hall as if plowing rows.
Snail woman. Mouth and small.

Beware the goodbye you forgot to say.
Handle with care or it will overtake
your garden with hungry mouths.

The garden will take root until
you go to snail. Then you too
will know how to pace and hum.

When you were here, we planted a garden.
I a fertile hole. When you left, aphids
took hold. Caterpillars too. I see them

from my window. Twists me in bed sheets
like a cold dream, mouth, hungry and small.

On "Near the Five Corners" by Kay Sage

I am my own figure. I can cut
a rug. Woman as in blood,
woman as in soft bones
and a mess of antlers.
You're near the five corners, but
you're not quite there. Do
you know what they are? Two
for each thigh. And one
for the corner in the middle.
You see architecture, but you
know nothing of middle corners,
how a body can turn around it
and go to pleasant static. How
my body is rainstick with
or without your touch.
You're not in the five corners. But instead,
you're in grid, as in chess, as in
graph paper, as in grate. I laugh
as you fumble, thick and lurid.

On "The Hidden Letter" by Kay Sage

To you I was mosaic, but
I wanted to be smooth dream.

On cool nights, you remember
me giddy and childlike in my

sleeping bag. You saw larva,
pupae, an act of becoming.

A mosquito was humming nearby,
one of three lives in the lilac desert.

You eat a little more cautiously
now, bulgy with middle age,

or perhaps because of when
I made oatmeal cookies

baked with glass.
You shouted through blood

Wretch, bitch, psycho. You
never understood this

is how I give of myself
more naked than sex.

And when you shower on
cold mornings, you think

of our first apartment,
how you ran the shower

to keep it warm. The light
in the bathroom was always

going out. You would
screw in a new bulb while

I held the cover like supplication.
Dead insects fell out.

I was holding up the sky.

When I left for the last time,
you would not look at me

as I consumed the doorway.
You were afraid of my face,

fingernail, hard and full of dirt.
But if you had, you would have seen

the hidden letter,
bigger than all chess pieces,

taller than god,
with curve, hollow and spite.

But one, whole thing.

On "Too Soon for Thunder" by Kay Sage

Because their organs move around so much,
horses get colic, and I think that is what
must be happening to me. Tangled gut.
I grow a hoof on top of my head.

My father had a horse once
he had to put down.
The other horses smelled the blood, after,
and wouldn't return to the barn.
Thirty years of trust, gone.
The other horses screamed.

I never asked my father
what the horse looked like,
after the mercy killing was done.

How much blood got on its skin?
What color was the hair against the red?
Did it look like it was sleeping,
except for the hole in its head?

On "The Giants Dance" by Kay Sage

(a Golden Shovel after Lana Del Ray)

Listen. The only way to swim is to kiss. /
There is no moving through, only towards. Me, /
I am a different size in water. I look hard /
at my refracted light. I am solid and wave. Before /
human beings ever floated. they were giants. You /
have legs that stretch to the bottom of the hot lake. I go /

stand on the edge on the last day of summertime /
and watch the other giants dance. This sadness /

is nostalgia for a moment that isn't done. I /
sputter in and out. I try to focus on swimming, and just /
jump like someone is taking a picture, like I wanted. /
I can feel my childhood ending. You /
only ache this way once. Once, everyone went out to /
play for the last time, but we didn't know /

it then. But I have swum at different sizes. I remember that /
all I have to do is trust I'll find other aches. As a baby, /
I swam, as a giant I swam. So you /
see, I jumped off that cliff, finally, seventeen, the /
largest swimmer, as big as the lake, where I fit best. /

On "Secret Voyage of a Spark" by Kay Sage

Sleeping over at a friend's,
you wait until the family
and other children are asleep
and slip out in
pajamas and bare feet. You
find the park in streetlight
and moon. You are trying
on shadow-person like a mask,
playing at cashiers who work in gas-stations
on highway towns or night
janitors at foreign hospitals.
On the swing, you think
time a photograph of motion.
You are all points of an arc.
There is no out and back—
you are everywhere elliptical.
You are the secret voyage of a spark.
All day-planners are works of fiction.
All voyages are your own.
You can go back. You are still there.

On "I Saw Three Cities" by Kay Sage

Neither living nor dead,
I saw three cities,
all without blood. I, too,
am bloodless, without heart
or motion. John or Nike,
I stand in the gray-green of a storm
that never comes.
In one of the cities,
I saw a death. A gun
as lidless as I am wrapped
in a woman's stiff hand.
A bullet folded through the fat
of her heart, as if she too were
pole and cloth. I will not tell you
what I saw in the other two cities.
Not the land of the dead,
but its twin. This is the place
where grief goes static.
Not the violence but the
dissociation after. A land
where no shadows move.
But see how my robe or shroud
is caught up in a wind that
must have blown. See how
I grew shoulders, almost, to bury
my lack of head so it can sob
without a mouth. Are still things
really still?

On "The Upper Side of the Sky" by Kay Sage

Here, you can see what love is.
The prosaic is far below. There
are no bills to pay, no eggs to carry,
and no diversions.
Trifurcated and before you,
you must make a choice.

The first is a yellow
and a fleeing. How your
lover is like coattails,
their body just out of reach.
The things you can do to
fruit when no one is looking.
The bright melon a stand-in
for real flesh and underwear.

The middle is a hinge
that doesn't go anywhere.
When folded in half, a body
become so solid, it no longer
feels corporal. Is that
what you thought the first
time I folded for you
on your bed? I hope
you didn't feel absence,
feel hole. I am not a sack
of meat; nothing leaks.
I am as certain as marble.

The third is a city. It goes
higher than the upper
limit of the sky. Is
this a place we can walk
together, holding hands?

Windowless and too high for pigment,
life goes watercolor.
It can wash away.

I do not know which one
is best. Love without touch,
touch without bodies, bodies
without life. Lover, all I want
is to write letters and get lost in
grocery stores. My heart
is not a bird but a frog. All I know is,
my favorite safe word is you.

On "Midnight Street" by Kay Sage

You told me as a child, everywhere
you went, you wore a raincoat.
With your father on trains,
with your mother at markets, no matter
the weather, you were your own shelter.
Your parents took you to the beach.
Over blue trunks and tennis shoes,
you made yourself a paper boy boat
anchored in sand. *What a child,*
your parents said, shaking their heads,
who refuses to get wet.

There was a sudden storm,
and you were airborne. A tarp
into sail. You were buffeted
and afraid. Further out to sea, you
bobbed, your parents screaming from the shore.
Twenty years later I saw you,
on a midnight street, otherwise I never
would have believed you. A little ghost
all the way blown to Roman cobblestone.

You told the story like all of yourself made it
home, like hours later your parents found you,
shivering but mostly dry.
You joked that the moral here is
don't wear a raincoat to the beach,
but if you do, wear a raincoat.

This is how love works. How stubbornly
we cling to foolishness, how we find
ourselves in green hills that go on
and on, a house built like a barn.

How we leave scaffolding
for something that moves.
If we end up killing each other,
at least we're not dying alone. Goodbye,

little ghost that brought me here.
Now neither of us will ever have to get wet.

On "In the Third Sleep" by Kay Sage

There are three sleeps that pull
us furthest through time. The first
is after passing meconium. Did
we think we were going back
to warmth and wet? We wake up
under bright lights and swaddles.
We raise our tiny fists to god.

We shared our second sleep,
although we did not know it at the time.
You took me to lunch in a small
restaurant and asked what if this
were our house? I said I'd put
the living room by the entrance
with space for dancing and my bed
behind double doors. You said
you'd sleep in the fountain
to save time by eliminating bathing.

Ashile, when you got home you called me
and asked when are we going to lunch.
My head was thick a nap and too much wine.
I cannot remember what I replied.
I hope it was as gentle as water.

You were a few days into the third sleep,
Kurt, when I knew. You skated
over ice in your coat,
my husband's rifle like the mast of a ship.
You pushed off for the land of nod,
set sail in one red smear.

Now I move in smaller circles,
frozen in telephone wires.
I shuttle back and forth between
sleeps. First, second, third, over
and back again. All three sleeps
have little mouths.
I caress them when I can.

On "Bounded on the West by the Land Under Water" by Kay Sage

Life can be a wound. Lake Natron in Tanzania
is red with algae scabbing the surface
in blooms. When bats, flamingos,
and eagles bump into water,
they go to stone. My whole life,

I have painted water incorrect—blue
and empty. I go back now with blood.
No, not blood but little plants that don't
need our sympathetic gaze. How inevitable
the crash of towers, how inevitable

a little life we can't capture
that stops mid-flight. My paint
is just brushstroke by an arm
still moving offstage. What you see
is a horizon in time, bounded

on the west by land under water.
In movies, if you see the actors
making plans, you know something
will go awry, but if it's left a mystery,
you know it will work. I am moving,

although I may look dead to you.
I am moving, although you won't
see a blink. I am moving, deep in
the red place, under water. Stillness,
what are you? A wound can be a life.

On "Festa" by Kay Sage

We are ninety percent water, but
we carry different things than the ocean.

I had only a handbag. My shape
did not stay in its container but

went to blown out skirt,
smear flower floating

while well-meaning onlookers
peered up inside.

When I was a child, I thought
the ocean could carry sound,

that you could shout *I love you*
to someone across the Atlantic, and if

you did it just right, they would hear.
It was only a matter of timing and patience.

But waves don't work like that,
the kind in oceans carry ships,

and I am no ship, am
passengerless. I drove myself,

party of one. Landlubbers, we have
driftwood on our mantelpiece and another

on the dresser. I do not love them;
they were just things that came with

deceased estate. Old, gnarled
like guts. It wasn't my stomach

that hurt but down below. Two
weeks late and then—

Water bears murk and scale.
Swimmy things, learning how to be soup.

They hooked me up. Two
IV bags that made me cold. Other

sicknesses brought me stew, or
when I couldn't eat, a handful of olives.

I liked eating around the pits. Water
carries messages in bottles,

quiet pleas for assistance. I had
hoped I would find one, someday.

The nurses had no news, not really.
Follow up, even if you're feeling better.

It wasn't the sort of thing they could test for.
And then I drove myself home,

eyes bald and wide like a gun. Ninety percent
water, and I couldn't carry a tune.

On "On the First of March, Crows Begin to Search" by Kay Sage

All animals wait, in their animal way—
the cicadas for seventeen years,
impossible and underground. We
thought the trees were screaming.

Spiders, too, are patient, becoming
fisher and line for whatever comes their way.
Turtles incubate to hatch before plodding to sea.
Our dogs wait to be fed.

But on the first of March, crows
begin to search. Is it you they
are looking for? I see them,
men in coats, bobbing and furtive.

I want to call it murder, when
a tunnel in the brain blows out. I could
tell the crows it's done, it's over.

Your body went to ash while
mine got fat on funeral casserole.
I grow tender with no gentleness.
I am all distended udder.

But let them, let the crows keep searching.
They have waited this long.

On "Ring of Iron, Ring of Wool" by Kay Sage

You find the end of the world
in a box of cigarettes, the yellow
tips lined up like soldiers.
You remember to turn a lucky.

At an art gallery, you
stand in an alley to smoke,
where the graffiti is vines going to guns.
A couple leaves, their arms around each other's waists,
towards the light at the other end.

A woman in a vest with dogs on it
takes out a plastic bag labeled *Biohazard*
and drinks something in vials.

You see it in flashes, like neon
panties through dress pants,
like something caught in teeth.
You see it in obstetrics waiting rooms,
behind a neglected fish-tank.

The end of the world refuses to use coasters.
When it sets its coffee down,
it leaves a ring of iron. Ring of wool
is how your mouth feels when
you speak its name.

You know no one will miss fish,
beasts, and birds,
when the end strikes by getting
in cracks and phone wires.
When all life goes to rubble,
who would mourn it?

What does it mean that the end
has a smaller, unplanned twin?
A boat mid-abortion.
You have seen it
between wafts of city-piss smell.
It's in the back. Does the
stillness make it impending
or the other way around?

On "The Seven Sleepers" by Kay Sage

Your body is a bag
folded around a tube.
Think of all the vacuum
cleaners left in closets.
They came out just fine.

We, seven sleepers,
can be more, if you like.
We took its skin off
then called it a god.
It will keep us safe.

On "All Surroundings Are Referred to High Water" by Kay Sage

I know now that lobsters are not immortal,
>but instead shed their exoskeletons when their flesh
bumps against it, like a toddler taking off
too-tight clothes. Each undressing
takes more time and energy as the lobster grows.
And because lobsters never stop growing,
they die sometimes, mid-eclosion,
of exhaustion. I see myself

as cathedral, getting knocked down
>and rebuilt, each clearing
of debris more laborious than the last.
I have to be careful when I bump against supporting
walls. You told me you collect

suicides because even that doesn't guarantee
>immortality. I wondered if you meant a scrapbook—
little things you made and found, turned sea-creature
with all the glue. A two-page spread with punch-outs
for Elliott Smith, globs of glitter for Marilyn.
Little construction-paper waves for Hart Crane
for when all surroundings were referred to high water.
I don't think you meant to be mawkish.
You would eat the suicides' transgressions
if you could, but instead you must store them another way.

As late as 1906, villages still had sin-eaters,
        wretches paid to ease the suffering of the dead.
        At the wake, a loved one would place a morsel
        of food on the departed's chest
        to absorb their sins, like sins were sauce or brine.
        After waiting—a few minutes? an hour?—
        the outcast would eat, each soul's passing
        made lighter by not having to carry
        what no longer fit them. Then the sin-eater
        became an outcast, forced to live
        outside the village, dreaded like an ominous building
        that must now and then be visited.

I know now that I am not immortal.
        I've known that for a long time.
        When I go, however I go,
        place a blue lobster on my chest.

On "Mother of Time" by Kay Sage

They're not scars,
because I won't stop picking:
The girl, the shopkeeper,
who smiled at my halting French,
wide-eyed boys, stuffed full
of chocolate and valor.
All will live a little less than I.

A woman in a wasps' nest made of paper bags.
tells me I've lived too long,
using gums now for soup.

She says this nest is bright spit out,
drafting papers, telegrams, wounds
from government offices.
She says, I am the mother of time.
I am war.

In my home, the wind pokes
through rain gutters,
the wind rattles the door.
I cannot take broom
to gray pustules under eaves.

Let the insects have their chorus.
Let the mother take me back.

On "Unicorns Came Down to the Sea" by Kay Sage

At the end of his life, Oedipus dreams
he is the Fisher King. Already,
he knows thigh wounds
and mists that spill out like sour milk
but knows nothing of down to the sea.
Perhaps he has pearls for eyes.

Eyes that were stabbed out by
hairpins, unicorn horns that fit
in fists made slippery from jam.
He casts his rod and waits for tug.

His mind is a mind that rests now,
only one question left
for poor travelers with aching feet.
A riddle set things in motion
but in this last reprieve,
an unknown question is the end
of fallow kingdom.

This is the shape that is waiting:
Blind man, old sins, dreaming
in different stories.
My eyes, too, went to fishy fog,
cataracts beyond surgeon's hunting.

In the twilight kingdom,
the kingdom of reeds and
princes afraid to pounce,
Oedipus feels a bite.

He wrenches in a trout,
bashes in head on empty
seat next to him. He touches
sea petals and salty bones.
Before waking, he says out loud
My mother is a fish.

III.

On "Starlings, Caravans" by Kay Sage

Once, I broke my own heart. Listen. Miscarriage is normal, expected, considered fine. We get our hopes up. We say, *Yes, yes, we can do this*. Our bodies know what to do.

Kay Sage is a painter with rules. I can't quite figure them out when I'm awake, which makes sense, is right, for a Surrealist. But observe *Unicorns Came Down to the Sea* and *All Surroundings are Referred to High Water*. They look similar, don't they? In fact, writing a poem for each, I had inadvertently switched them. Both have the color pallet of the Mediterranean. I've spent a few months there. The Mediterranean, I mean, not the paintings. Greece and Rome. You hear folks who pretend to be worldly go on about that light, that yellow, drowsy light, but they're not wrong.

At my past job, my boss would tell me I didn't observe well. I think she thought I had a learning-disability. Everything I did had tiny typos or miscalculations. I would say, *I thought it was okay to make mistakes*. And she would say, *No, not like this*.

*

Hysterical pregnancies are also normal enough. Maybe it's just in old-timey novels and sitcoms, though. I've taken pregnancy tests at Target. Once, at Braum's. I got a burger after.

A month ago, I set myself up to have something small, nonexistent die. I had a hysterical miscarriage. There isn't a name for it. That's what I call it. It sounds unimportant and kind of funny. The doctors certainly thought so.

I like to think I can see things, though, like straight to the bones of things. This couch I am writing on is blue. I couldn't remember if the sides had studs on them or not and had to look again. They do.

But what I do know is the way it fits my body. The back, it feels overstuffed, like it's pushing on me, but the base of my spine is cradled, and I don't feel any of its old aches.

A month ago, I was late. Two weeks. And then, the sensation of stabbing. Of falling.

Elliott Smith stabbed himself in the chest. Not once, but twice.

In the cult I was raised in, I was taught no one was cursed. We can all be redeemed. Depression was a choice and didn't have to be terminal. I know the first part is a lie, but I find myself struggling with the second. It seems inevitable that Kay Sage shot herself in the chest, doesn't it? I mean, look at her paintings, all are the moment before the gun goes off and the moment after. That's how you know there isn't a way out.

Almost all of her paintings have architectural elements in them. Little structures that could exist, but don't. Nothing in hospitals is that inevitable, that still. Things in real life can feel looming, but don't actually hover. You, the viewer, are God, seeing things straight on.

Her paintings have draped cloth, sometimes in human form, but more often statues of what human beings would be if they were headless. Her paintings are controlled. They are places you would like to visit but not places you would want to live. There was a breeze, but you just missed it.

*

The stabbing sensation was below. I interrupted my boss's meeting and said I have to go. My boss asked if I needed an ambulance. Well, what she said was *Are you okay to drive?* and I said *Yes*.

I bled through my pants on the drive over. The blood washed out, easy enough, the next day, which was good, because I just bought the pants, and I liked them. The next week, hiking with my husband, down a closed trail, they got ruined. I still have burrs in them. The pants are on top of a bucket of shoes in my closet.

Like all good painters, Sage breaks her own rules. Take *Starlings, Caravans,* for instance. The colors are purplish like clouds. The yellows are bright. It doesn't look like the town my father-in-law described before and after a tornado went through. So still, so waiting.

Underneath my body is a skeleton. I like to think it serves me. It gets me to the gym well enough. I like the row machine the best. Put this massive ass on a hard seat that other asses have sweated into. Use femurs and tibia to push it back and forth. Hold on with finger bones, phalanges. Your skeleton knows how to make a rhythm, even if you always clap on the 1's and 3's, and your musician husband teases you for it.

My hip bones are wide. The space between is empty, is filled with blood, tissue, fat.

*

At the hospital, no one was at the front desk. When they found me in the waiting area filling out paperwork I had helped myself to, they asked what was wrong. I said *I don't know what is happening. I think I'm having a miscarriage.* They asked how far along I was. I said *I don't know, I don't know.*

The tornado is happening now in *Starlings, Caravans.* A boat is ready. Oars are everywhere, scattered without deliberation.

Scholars tend not to read into Sage's titles, which is fair enough for a Surrealist painter. But I don't think it is a coincidence this one is called *Starlings, Caravans*. Things that move in groups.

Migration is only considered migration when it happens in groups. When World War II broke out, Sage paid for Surrealist ex-pats to flee from Europe. She arranged the passage. Then, Andre Breton kicked her out of the group for being too moneyed, too female, too privileged. This too, feels like breaking the rules.

*

At the hospital I peed in a cup. Not pregnant. I had two IV bags. They made me feel cold. The female doctor and the male nurse told me how periods work. That they hurt sometimes. I am 29 years old. I have had over 200.

The cult wasn't terribly interesting. The leader, hilariously, was also named Jim Jones.

But what stuck with me the most, besides the praying in tongues, the faith healers, the obsession with the year 2000—they called it a jubilee year—was how they treated young girls. When I was ten, I got my first period. We had to go to a prayer meeting. The next month, it came early, mid-prayer meeting. I asked my friend for a pad (tampons were taboo). She didn't have one. So we asked my mom for one. She told my father what was happening so she could get the keys and go to the store. Everyone was angry with me. *She's too young for this,* they said.

In *Starlings, Caravans* the perspective is different than in her other paintings. You, the viewer, are lower than the structures, gazing up into it, like someone being gurneyed into an ambulance. Or, to borrow a phrase from St. Vincent, *a birth in reverse.*

I want to believe in this painting and its painter. I was to believe her suicide was not inevitable. But what to say of the commotion while it is happening?

I don't always observe where my body is, running into protruding parts of the room, head in another space. I stubbed my toes on the couch. But I don't forget my bones.

*

I got Eve's curse. So do most people born with uteruses, at one time or another, but me in particular.

The cult taught us that once someone hit puberty, it was okay to tell their father that boys are going to be knocking down their door. You shouldn't wear a bra if you were still in middle school because you were too young. Your body moves over to adulthood slowly then all at once, and it better be a migration on time with everyone else in your grade. If you left childhood too early, something was wrong.

No one was cursed, except each and every girl, to carry a shame between her legs. No sin cannot be undone except puberty.

*

At the hospital, I thought about stingrays. There is no way they're not filled with love. I know projecting yourself onto the natural world is a kind of violence, perhaps even a violation, some sort of human-centered distortion. But how can I not observe the world through a human lens? So, think of it, gentle kites, in oceans, in far-off places, floating with more grace than you ever could.

The cult reduced me to a hole, I felt, a hole for a baby to pop out of, a hole to leak. *You, idiot hole, you idiot hole,* I would say before going to bed. And the hole was for men, too, or one man, who was your husband, unless it was Jesus. And this, too, was inevitable. You would grow up, properly, not too soon, marry a God-fearing man, have children. The children would live in a neighborhood somewhere in the Southwest, together, and have fellowship, community.

And if that didn't happen, it was because you were cursed (no one is cursed). When I left for college, didn't come back, lived with my boyfriend, left him, married an agnostic, and somewhere in there my mother tried to kill herself, no doubt the elders whispered, *See, see, of course this would happen.*

*

When you're bleeding, crying, hooked up to an IV bag, and pretending this doesn't make you feel cold, it's hard to convince the staff you're not prone to hysterics. That when you say this is the worst pain you've been in in your whole life, this includes getting in two accidents that total your car. That this includes someone breaking your tailbone. This includes getting stabbed.

Once, I saw a stingray's skeleton in a picture. They have a skeleton under there. The shock of it. Bones fanning out like oars. But I should have guessed that one: kites have cross beams. Muntins, I think they're called, but maybe that's just for windows.

The skeleton was indisputable. Beneath blubber and grace, hardened calcium. Just like particle board inside the couch, a defect in the brain, a tailbone.

But there wasn't a baby. The hospital confirms this. It's not that there was a baby that went away. There never was one to begin with. That it was just you, your brain convinced that all you could ever bring about was death.

On "This Is Another Day" by Kay Sage

Neither human nor animal,
all screams must go to the screaming place.
Shakey dome alone the crumbling beach.
Once they escape the teeth
(the youngest bones)
out they float like balloons
or bad perfume. They wander
until they find the nest.
Terrible birds with human irises.

Screaming is only screaming
once it crosses over.
At night, a coyote eats a cat—
it sounds like a child.
And when I was fifteen, I heard
a girl from a stuck place
keening in a high school bathroom.
Two teachers like sentinels
firmly escorted her out.

I have seen that cage made from
ancient bones, as still and quiet
as cadavers, flag made out of meat.
Coward, I turned away.

All I wanted was to get mine back,
every gasp, every little death
expelled for love of you.
I will begin again tomorrow.
Is another day also one for shrieking,
on and on like a bruised horse,
like loss is a word with a hole in it?

On "Tomorrow, Mr. Silber" by Kay Sage

(a Golden Shovel after Rebecca Sugar)

You always loved that *still* goes both ways. Time /
and place become stains. Is it any wonder your home is /
a museum of obscure sorrows? I stayed an /
eternity. Broken cameras, dusty carousels. Illusion /
of past obscene grandeur. I want that /
back, because, the next day, you died. It helps /
to remember you as Mobius strip. things /
a math that moves without moving. Make /
the shape from your old film strips. But I sense /

futility in superimposition. So /
I try, instead, to go inside your pictures we're /
worrying apart with our fingers. Always /
it is this way—dying as if living /
and back again. When we were together, in /
that pause, what was moving, and what was still? The /
actions and objects get jumbled in memory. Present /
past and future. Are they verb or noun tense? /

And a thousand years from now, your house, it /
goes to bones and ash, the earth scaffolding, seams /
down to threads, the wind unforgiving. /
The color of your film strips blocks the sun. When /
God made you still for a final, a /
long time, I said *You get what you love. Good.* /
I don't know how I feel now. This thing /
I carry, like a rare fruit, your absence, your ends /

and means at keeping still. But /
I twitch. I unravel. I move you. /
I cannot help but fold you around and /
twist you up. I cannot let you stay. And in my house, I /
clean assiduously. I rearrange. I will /

nouns and verbs to motion. Always /
I dust, I scrub, with mathematical precision. Be /
a Mobius film strip, over and back. /
Maybe death can't catch me if my favorite word is *then*. /
You and I will always be back then.

On "The Instant" by Kay Sage

My magic is in keeping still.
That is why people love the ocean.
They cannot move it, only take
parts of it with them home.

You thought my rigidity made me corpse
and you a magician, because
anything is possible with a canvas.
You threw knives at me, then

sliced my stomach. In this instant,
the audience gasped to see a trunk
like a tree felled. My intestines had
no rings, but undigested bricks,

copper piping, boat, and paneling.
But I don't have time for guests
or other sorts of spectacle.
My stillness is not for you.

Take a bow. Leave me half
a woman, no stranger than the sea.
When no one is looking, I will pull
a hat out of a rabbit that is invisible.

On "Small Portrait" by Kay Sage

To be a woman is like this now.
Scrub it off as if it were a stain—
all traces of your face.
Use bleach if you must or dish soap
if you have time to scrub.
You'll know when to stop.
The lattice where your nose
used to be won't hang vines or
go inside pianos. The cloth
won't swaddle any infants
or stifle any urges.
You are no longer meat dumpling,
no pleasant little pouch.
You are sad machine.
Do you remember the toy store
you went to as a kid?
One day, the Jack-in-the-Box
turned inside out when jerked
too fast, too far. All springs and
splay. This is you now.
And yet without eyes and mouth
and nose, you are not beyond reproach.
You thought machine indelible,
but they are saying you're mid-twitch.
A woman should not shudder in fear or orgasm.
A woman with or without a face should not move.
The only good victim is a corpse.

On "Song of Sevens" by Kay Sage

i go to the beach of broken
and sing the song of sevens
one part is for the sand
another for the waves
one for the moon
two for the gulls
the baritone for the wind
the high notes are for me

you have no room in this song
after i am done singing
i will fill my pockets with sand dollars
backs smashed in and pile

up my doorway
this is my ode to divorce
my small ceremony
for keeping safe

How to Give: On "Page 49" by Kay Sage

Not
the
asshole
but

above it is a cap like one for fuel.
I reach back and turn it counterclockwise
to open the little door that's at the root of all spines.
I use both hands with bent elbows and grab it.
The base is cold and metal like a skewer through a carousel horse.

I inhale. I yank it out.

It goes haltingly—

vertebra by vertebra,

like a locomotive,

one car at a time.

My breathing will be unlabored

like soothing mutters

on a quiet night.

My breathing will be all exhales

without that spider umbrella

of bone between.

I must do this to be weightless.

I must do this to be as water

that never thinks of itself,

but flows and heals and

asks nothing.

I must do this for the give.

And afterward, we could

prop it in some corner,

like a coatrack for small coats

or give it to the children

for a curious plaything.

I am trying to trade

my strength for kindness.

(It has taken me years to begin this, coming to it too late,
on the second-to-last page. Forgive me; it is the life-long task
of self to let go of scaffolds.)

On "The Outline of Silence" by Kay Sage

1. Strip excess foliage from flowers and cut stems to desired length (no shorter than six inches). To help flowers retain their color during the drying process, make sure to remove them from sunlight as soon as they're cut. Hang flowers individually or rubber-band stems together to hang a bouquet like a spider hangs a fly.

Consider the dung beetle. A small creature, given to extraordinary feats. Our reaction is somewhere between *Wow* and *Oh dear*, which is where most human reactions lie, if we gave anything enough pause.

Dung. Lowly, earthy, essential, universal. Industrial, hard-shelled soldiers take what is left and build homes.

We, of course, could never live in such places. We can picture ourselves a bee, a beautiful, hard-working bee, making something intricate and sweet. Or even a spider—noiseless and patient, cunning. But never in a dung-home.

Home. What a big word. How much does it weigh? In Ancient Greek, there was a word that means a journey home by sea: *Nostos*. Think *The Odyssey*. Odysseus was gone for so long, faced trials, and then came back. How nice, how linear. But it is interesting that he had to leave again. It very much ended with him leaving again. He will meet the people who have never seen the sea and tell them what it is like. He will bring an oar.

Kay Sage's *Outline of Silence* moves like a husk that was always a husk. Like someone looking back right at the moment of transformation. No, not their own transformation but someone else's. I looked back and you were turning into a tree. I looked back, my eyes didn't strain too far, but I saw you turning into salt.

Here, Odysseus might say, *Imagine the sands are water. You've seen the puddles after the rare rainfall. Imagine that but bigger. However large you are imagining the puddle, do that but more. That is what stands between you and home.*

*

But if you had to live in dung, consider your options. There's dung from herbivores and dung from omnivores, for one thing. The lowly beetle prefers the omnivores. I don't know why. But I read that, and I thought it sounded right.

And it's good to do something useful. Dung beetles take shit and recycle it and benefit the land. Grassland, wetland, desert—there is nothing that cannot be improved by small builders, making homes out of dung.

Anne Carson wrote once that you can make history a thing that carries itself. Your home and your history—are they not the same thing? It is impossible to think of your history without thinking of childhood homes. I worry about the state of mine. My parents keep cramming it full of more and more junk. My mother sleeps in what used to be my bedroom.

My father will refuse a nursing home, and my mother will stay with him. I can imagine the house collapsing, years of delayed repairs. All the tools turning into trash. For years, my parents didn't fix the leak in my sister's bedroom. A drip through the sheetrock made bubbles like volcanoes.

2. Find a dark, dry area with good circulation, such as an attic or unused closet. Use the sort of place that one would hang themselves in if they ever got the urge. With unflavored dental floss, secure the bottom of the flowers' stems to a hanger so that they hang upside down to dry. Any kind of small string will do the trick, actually. I used twine on my sunflowers from my wedding. Leave flowers for two to three weeks until completely dry.

There are several species of dung beetle. There are burrowing dung-beetles, chiefly in parts of Africa. They go to a pile of, you know, a pile of dung and burrow tunnels. Stippling it. Blasting something full of light.

And of course, there is the rolling dung beetle type. They don't burrow into mounds of shit with their families. They take segments—I saw this on a nature documentary—and roll it. Like Sisyphus in reverse. On and on until they get a ball of it. And they carry someone else's shit on their back. Like the sin-eaters of old, they get called dirty, disgusting, for doing what must be done to keep the world in balance.

Looking at the painting now, I moved my left arm in front of my chest and splayed my hand out in paralyzed reaching, an awkwardly balanced pose. *No, no, don't do that,* meaning myself but someone else as well.

In the middle of the painting, we see what appears to be a cloth tumbling over scaffolding, in red, white, and sulfur green, which is standard for a Kay Sage painting. We see paralyzed force without gesture.

Silence is always on the end of something else. Silence must always have an outline. It cannot be boundless, even if you don't see the edges.

3. Remove flowers from hangers and spray with unscented hairspray for protection from time and other disrupters of plans.

In Arizona, it doesn't rain too often, but every August, there are monsoons. Leftovers from tropical storms that knock out the power and force buckets of rain through shitty roofs, over collections of stamps, over model trains, CB radios, rooms piled with unread books.

In *Outline of Silence.* did Sage mean a silent band you carry with you, like a talisman, or did she mean the hem of a vast, immovable silence? The former sounds like peace, the latter is threatening. I think Sage meant both.

And that is what it means to have a home, a history that does and does not carry itself. It'll keep you safe—a little shelter of soft, like tumbling laundry against scaffolding you could fall through. And something looming in the background, like a monsoon, you can only see its shape.

And so, Odysseus might add, *the sea is a history, and in my telling, I have brought you a piece.*

I know that when writing a lyrical essay, you're supposed to end on the tonic, hit the note you started on, make it one big ball. But I wake up crying for no reason—everything feels heavy and far away. My breath smells terrible, and I drink more than I should. Sometimes I know the floor is slanted but cannot decide if it's slanted up or slanted down. So, I just want to tell you this: In Africa, there is a dung beetle, and it is the only insect known to navigate by star.

On "Nests of Lightning" by Kay Sage

Here, it is October all year.
I wake before dawn
—usually around seven—
and tend my small garden of tubers,
rake leaves from under the lattices.
In afternoons (and in October
it is always afternoon) I nap.
I drink water from coffee mugs.

Living this way is like tending
nests of lighting, hoping a hatch
never happens, puttering around
in the time of wooden ghosts.

You sent me a photo
of your infant son,
swaddled in a hospital blanket
in the back seat. You wrote
For Linus, it is always raining,
and I wept.

On "Unusual Thursday" by Kay Sage

The laundry sat with bits of bone
or dinner on the lawn. Books and cloth
could be anything in the morning light.

////

A bridge waits for you to cross it.
You don't know how to begin.
You long for ladders only.
You want to swim up there.

///

(((I hate seeing you in our bed,
body curved like a clove
of garlic, echoing the place
my body could go.)))

///

My nightstand has an empty
glass. I thought it would feel better
with you nearby. My small
gestures at love.

///

Thursday, the trash goes out.
I will put my clothes and parts
of house out there and apologize.
I hope they learn to swim.

///

Before you, I was alone.
I've worked so hard. Am
I building or decreating?
All I know is, I am still alone.
But it is better now, somehow.

On "Reflex Arc" by Kay Sage

Movement is brutal.
At each moment, a thousand short shocks.
Even when still, the reflex arc
sparks—reflective muscles contract,
organs jitter.

Growing up, we had a carousel,
the kind for pictures. Click
click click went the screen
until it froze mid-transition.
This is you now.

Be still was what I thought,
flinching at every disaster.
And I have tried, in confessionals
and half-spun libraries. I held
my self like loom, like scaffold,
like vessel waiting.

Be still is where you go when body
is breaking. I rethink when you did it,
as if endless repetition can be a sort
of still. A low hum of images
until you go to blur—which is
another word for stuck.

Growing up, we had a carousel,
the kind for pictures. Click
click click went the screen
until it froze mid-transition.
This is you now.

And this poem, this poem
is not a souvenir.

On "Men Working" by Kay Sage

In Rome, on subways, I laid my arms
    on the backs of seats,
        imagining they could extend
            through the cars like cord through
    spine,
      fingertips brushing darkness.
    Along the Nile, I focused
my swimsuit away, then my skin.
    I am particle, I am wave.
        In the Midwest, I did my best work.
           I dug out my quilt and draped
      it around me all year.
I stood in the sun until
I too was bleached patchwork.
    I wanted landscape only,
        something for you to paint
           that didn't gaze back.
    I wanted to escape
all notice, especially by men.
Working assiduously at invisibility,
    I still fell short.
        I almost hated you for it.
           You told me that before we met,
    you had *dreamed*
of a lighthouse in the woods,
of a glass of water *with a big slice of lemon.*

On "A Short Day" by Kay Sage

i am a drifter
temporarily
inconvenienced
the house and husband
were by accident

youll see
the holes
will come back
a wood rot
up the stairs
a hesitation before
a laugh
a sunburned lip

i looked like a statue
in your shirt
on your rowboat
you learned
i am more
than soft hole
mouth to ass
you learn of annex
i am the shrug
that cares without caring
i am as heavy as clouds

being loved feels
like bathrooms
everything present
a body turns to toilet
just a thing to ache into

my whole life is nylon
the ladder is hidden
at my thigh

the holes are contagious
will be like termites
turn it to lace
turn it into lattice
turn this home into reeds

its not coming its waiting
the space between atoms
expanding
and none of it
none of it will be soft

On "The Point of Intersection" by Kay Sage

I will bake bread,
and share it with you,
because when you were a kid,
you felt like a ghost in your house.
Is it any wonder you could float?

At night, while the heavy ones slept,
you glided through the kitchen
in socks and pajama bottoms,
stood on furniture, and took
because you could. You said

you only saw the backs of things,
then—like seeing the pages
but not the spine, or the ear part
but not the disc.

I don't know what's on the other side.
My heart is more Mobius than Euclid.
But I know what it means for two lines
to have a point of intersection.
If the plane is flat, one flash then separation.

But if on a curve, a twist of paper,
one will come back always, but
sea-changed, and on the back,
on the back of things.

I don't know if it's odd
or even this time or if it's me
or you that's upside down now,
but digestion works from all angles.
And you baked bread
and will share it with me.

On "On the Contrary" by Kay Sage

All flying begins with peeling.
From egg to bird, cocoon to butterfly,

and less noble scratchings.
People write about bursting

into flight—what rush—
but, I have seen the slow slough

of age. Dirt and skin, too,
go airborne, and have little

flurries of their own.
I have seen twinned flight,

on an airplane to America.
No, not twins, father and son.

Tell me: Did they ever find the body?
Did the feathers work for floating?

All I knew of flight
I learned from windows and death.

On "Dreamy Cars for Waterbury" by Kay Sage

A whale swims differently than a fly.
The oxygen cycles slower but the animal
covers more ground. For a planet,
a thousand years goes by in a blink.
For an atom, a day is an eternity.
But that night, all things were the same size,
my head on your shoulder in the back of a cab
the night the paint started to thin.
All things swam the same direction—
it was all dreamy cars for Waterbury.
Everyone was in pajamas weeping.
Even the buildings wore bedsheets.
Ahead was someone we half-remembered.
We'll never get out in time.
(But what a beautiful bowl above your breast,
for empty head that nods and nods
and pretends the night will last forever,
that all life can be a wistful elegy
for night-films and one-way cabs.)
Of course, the figure will approach us,
buzz towards us like a fly to fruit,
as ponderous as a whale,
if not tomorrow then in a thousand years.
Its sheets are the size of America.
And I already know what it will ask mouthless:
Tell me, with the shudder of your gun,
is your breath going in or out?

On "Third Paragraph" by Kay Sage

This is the kingdom of having lost
animals, doors blown open, searching
a quiet street where you feel
foolish calling out names.

Always, there is walking,
first frantic then methodical,
at the end, a partial ritual so you can say
you looked and looked well.

Between the blue and green
doors, you see your house,
the one you used to have.
It's in another town, but you can see it.

A lamp is on, eggplant-shaped
and purple. A world
of round, sunset,
and contained light.

You remember the pine
branches used to scrape
your roof on windy nights.
They sounded like birds.

In the lost animal kingdom,
the streets are scentless,
nothing is lurking. You
arrive there with no preamble,

like coming into a description
of what it means to thirst.

On "No Passing" by Kay Sage

All liminal journeys come to an end,
a point through which there is no passing.
I have pillow imprints on my cheeks.
Death isn't what it used to be.
I would know. I've been there before.

I have come to an end,
a journey through which there is no passing.
I have point pricks on my cheeks.
Pillows aren't what they used to be.
Death would know. Death has been here before.

All death has come to an end.
I am that which there is no passing.
I have pillow imprints on my journeys.
My points aren't what they used to be.
My cheeks would know, having been there before.

All pillows come to an end.
Death there is no passing.
I have my own imprints on the inside of my cheeks.
Journeys aren't what they used to be.
I don't know the point of changing.

All points come to an end,
a pillow through which there is no passing.
I have death imprints on my cheeks.
I am not what I used to be.
Journeys are not just for the unknown.

IV.

On "A Bird in the Room" by Kay Sage

The year after you died, I refused all fruit.
I could not bear that hybrid of plant and ghost.
By the time a lemon reaches the east coast,
its tree could be in flames.
All that's left a sour ball,
a seed unwelcome on chicken.

The month you died, I kept the fruit
I found on walks in shadows.
If I can't have it, no one will.
I stuck them in my rafters,
where darkness transformed them.
Not castration but refuse.

The week you died, I examined pits.
Nectarines, apricots, peaches,
all malformed brains. I had wondered
about mangoes. Under sunset skin,
thick, orange slime. What keeps
their roundness? Can you read braille?

The day you died, there was a bird
in the room. Round and pulsing,
a bird is a kind of fruit. You
can take it apart with your hands.
I think it was looking for a tree
filled with pomegranates or twigs.

I know what the old women say:
If a bird enters your home, a member
of your household will die. I did not know
they meant the spot where all gentleness gathers,
the pit. You have to wonder the causality
and how far back it will go.

The year I refused fruit made me still
inside, the stillness filled our house
with grey. The pits fell out of rotting
bodies. The bird got lost somehow
and invited itself in. I think it killed you,
love, killed you with feathers and legs.

How perverse that you will never go
into the ground, never go to tree.
You'll fly, little bird, out over the coast.
But I will leave my door open for you
in case you get lost. For you, love,
I will fill my home with ash.

On "Day Without Name" by Kay Sage

At Bible study, you read about Thomas. The other kids snickered at his unbelief. You thought of his worker hand, gliding into a wound, like a knife into fish. What did it touch after? Did he wipe it on his tunic, God blood on old rags? Did the smear come out in the wash?

The image lost its resonance over the years. Your own gash allows neither entry nor egress. You don't think a body can come back after it becomes wended into wood.

Sometimes you find small rocks. You like the ones with holes. You put your whole hands in geodes, careful not to chip your nails, which are bitten to death anyways. The rock reminds you your doubt, too, is a way to a gory miracle.

On "The Circle Never Sleeps" by Kay Sage

i am trying to hold
and remain invisible like
north holds a needle
or vessels hold blood.
i call you up and you say
youre doing partial hospitalization.
five hours a day you go to group
at carrollton springs because
last monday you were feeling
suicidey so you emailed your psychiatrist
and said you were feeling suicidey
(suicidal sounded too dramatic)
and two hours of waiting later
and a whole lot of paperwork
there you are. big bang theory
is playing in the waiting room
and your husband says this is worse
than the shoe you threw at him.
you tell me all this walking your dog
friday night. im on my way to
a birthday party in richardson. shes
a good dog hes a good husband.
you say im a good friend too
for going to this birthday party for a friend
we are both a little upset with. i say
i dont know the etiquette of this situation but
well im sorry for your loss.
i say at least itll grow back.
and i am that laugh before you sob.
i am the patron saint of
peter pans tom sawyers and other innocent lowlifes.
saturday i go to judys cafe ii
and the duncanville public library
being in the mood for worn down places.

i go to oak cliff for coffee. a family
sits on lawn chairs outside a gas station.
the brown father holds a white sign
that says HARD TIMES PLEASE HELP.
i buy cigarettes a large bottle of water
and five bananas. i feel awkward and
look at my shoes. i dont know the etiquette
of this situation. i hand the bag
to the father but stick the cigs in my pocket.
god bless you the father says the mother
too. the baby reaches for a nipple.
its fall again and i just feel
like crying. the circle never sleeps.
leaving oak cliff i see the profile of a man
standing on top of bank of america. far enough
away even atlas goes to line.
hold, hold, hold.
the city is latte and overripe.
hold, hold, hold.

On "Signal to Signal" by Kay Sage

SIGNAL: Once, I had an imaginary friend, but I forget their name.
SIGNAL: Once, I could make myself small.
SIGNAL: Once, I had enough of holes and other openings.
SIGNAL: And you thought only of glue.
SIGNAL: Glue, and other fixatives. Like staples, tape, and thumbtacks.
SIGNAL: You were trying to find out about color and what makes it stick.
SIGNAL: Stick to the back of things.
SIGNAL: You looked for hangings like on paintings, you touched with hands like rabbits, looking.
SIGNAL: Yes, I couldn't find anything. What makes the yellow on me refuse to slough off? Even the wind can't get it.
SIGNAL: No, not even the wind.
SIGNAL: Once, I had an imaginary friend. The sex was no good, so they left.
SIGNAL: Now, you don't think of colors, only holes.
SIGNAL: Openings. Hard and soft.
SIGNAL: Are dreams a hard or soft opening?
SIGNAL: Soft, soft like cloud wisps or things caught in windows.
SIGNAL: Do you miss them?
SIGNAL: Who?
SIGNAL: Your friend, I mean.
SIGNAL: You never talk any sense.
SIGNAL: I had a friend once, they were thousands of feet tall. Their head brushed the moon, it used to be closer in those days.
SIGNAL: Those were the days, weren't they?
SIGNAL: What color was the moon? How did it get on there?
SIGNAL: A doorway brought white to the moon.

On "This Silent World" by Kay Sage

You were a poor man, who
knew but a little, until
suddenly, you knew more
than Adam. Did that knowledge
burst like umbrellas or fester
like mushrooms in secret places?

When you stumbled
out four days later, into
this silent world, were
you astonished or yawning
after a little sleep?
Did the world yawn with you,
rocks like teeth, the ground
a shudder-grey?

I go to that place. I choose it.
Black like the insides of eyelids,
black like dirt under fingernails,
black like recalling a dream too
late, the color of slipping.
Did you see me there? We lived
and died about two thousand years
apart, but did you know no life,
no narrative is a straight line,
especially those who choose bullets
for punctuation?

Did you learn geometry in school?
You probably didn't go.
I made rays first, then paintings,
going right to left. I have no note
for you, only notes for the end

of useless light. But, fellow
tomb-dweller, while you were in
the blackened place, did you hear my song?

O Lazarus, I have questions
and answers for you too

I haven't come back yet
but when I do

You'll all go shadow-waltzing
in your Sunday blues

On "Tomorrow Is Never" by Kay Sage

We'll put them out to sea. They are
quiet and smell of hair on pillow.
We won't even bother with food.
They can catch gull and whale,

although they are soft-bodied
and gummed. We know how
they can devour. Behind cages
and out to sea, their tomorrow is never

our problem. No matter that animals
now alarm. No matter that now
our bones feel stippled with cancer,
and film covers our eyes.

We'll just put them out to sea. They are
quiet, but so are stains and scars. We'll
try not to sail past them, because if we do
we'll feel we've swallowed pieces of moon.

On "Le Passage" by Kay Sage

Twigs and broken lungs
are the same here—
a space for something
to be furthered or complete
but isn't. Everyone has
their preferences. *Phantasmaphile*
they called me and worse.
Take your fetish for rubber
and apply it to your whole
life. I find calm in staring
at blocks that could be anything.
They stretch out like the sea.
You wouldn't love me if
I turned to face you. Look
instead at my golden head.
It glows as if ordained. Do
not speak. What you could
say outstrides what you will.
I have the back of a scalpel.
Sleep for dinner, wait for rain.

On "Suspension Bridge for the Sparrows"
   by Kay Sage

I wanted to love you
like doing up buttons:
to take up completely
and then be still.

On "South to Southwesterly Winds Tomorrow" by Kay Sage

I am dumb and heavy
and not at all like the ginkgo tree.
The leaves fan out like a two-headed
boy I saw in a museum once—
two faces attached by jaw.
The trees go in pairs too, male and female
with acorns and ovum. The branches
are high, punctuated by light.
Their genome has more than ten
times the DNA pairings than we do.
It is no surprise, then, they survived
Hiroshima, atoms holding firm
to bark, roots, and leaves.
All one place, not moving.

*

I am dumb and heavy,
and not all like your beehives,
motion pressing into light. I thought
they were filing cabinets given
over to hill and brush, but you said
to come closer and I will show you
not you, a hundred thousand not you.
When a beekeeper dies, you must tell
the bees when the ground is still fresh.
But all over, the workers are leaving,
and there is no ceremony for that.
I take my leavings slow, and leave
no sweetness, no remembrances of light.

*

I am dumb and heavy, and not at all
like filing cabinets in police back offices,
filled up with cards of missing children.
On Christmas Eve, five siblings stay up,
too excited to sleep. Their other four siblings go to bed.
Their mother answers the telephone late at night.
A man's voice asks for someone
no one has heard of. Then the voice laughs
and hangs up. The mother thinks she
hears footsteps on the roof,
but doesn't think anything of it.
The house with twelve people inside
catches on fire, and the five siblings who
had stayed up all disappear.

*

I have tried to find things to
ache into, like putting down a hearty root
or pouring honey from a box,
or leaving a record no one believes or reads.
But nothing fits into grief frames. They
hang empty and overhead like unblinking
vultures. South to southwesterly winds
tomorrow will blow them away, no doubt,
and nothing will be left of my face.

On "Detour" by Kay Sage

I am taking a detour to explain what I am doing. The book is almost over, but a year and a bit later, I just now figured out what I have been trying to say.

After losing her husband to a sudden brain aneurysm, Sage shot herself in the heart. And I've been thinking about what shape a suicide makes.

Take a look at the painting *Detour,* one of Sage's last works. In the distance, lines converge and fan out towards us, the viewers. There's an end point, we can see it, but as the lines reach back, there's no real beginning, at least, not one we can see. And that, I think, is what suicide looks like to me: one point (definite) but it triggers an arrow—backwards through time.

Let me try again. Suicide seems like a fixed object. This triggers something reaching back through time. Like the geometric figure of a ray you learned about in geometry, but instead of in space, in time.

I'm not saying Sage's or anybody's suicide is inevitable. Depression is not a fatal disease, right? But it sure does seem like it to those left behind.

That fixed point reshapes the past, and we have to re-think how we understood the person who died that way. That is what I was trying to say in these poems, prose poems, two essays, one dialogue.

Except not so simple. Regular geometry presumes a flat surface. But in a saddle-shaped plane, parallel lines meet. So then, if suicide is a ray, what plane is it on?

Thinking up this prose detour while driving, I kept trying to remember the word for *Mobius Strip,* but my tired brain kept going *tardigrade* and then *Wait, no, that's an animal.* I'm not sure why, although I'm not very bright in the mornings. Perhaps because I wrote a poem four years ago for a friend and used the image of a tardigrade dying—how unexpected, how the opposite of what we thought would happen, until it became *of course.* Perhaps because if anyone could survive a Mobius strip, it's a tardigrade.

At any rate, a Mobius strip works handily enough. Take a strip of paper and make a loop. That's the practice. Now undo the loop then try again, this time putting a twist in it. You can do any odd-numbed of loops. And there you have it: One-sided paper. Or do it again, but with a strip of paper or ribbon with an up-down oriented pattern. (I pictured a ribbon I had as a child with a sheep repeated on it.) Now make the strip again. Where the paper or ribbon meets itself, one sheep is upside down. Transformed, twinned.

A gun goes off on January 8th, 1963. And this defined point causes events in Sage's life to take shape. And that shape is a tardigrade—tough and adaptable. Sometimes, the shape is hibernating but will come back, again and again. That shape is a clone of itself, one for every moment. Sometimes, that animal is upside down, all eight legs wriggling.

On "The Answer Is No" by Kay Sage

Things left undone can become
a city, further out,
and have little lives of their own.

Mold blooms in teas you never tried.
Poems you meant to write paper a bathroom.
You are somewhere in that
city of unhemmed garments.

The answer is *no* to a complicated question
I cannot bear to ask.
How *no* can become white noise
after a while, when uttered enough times.

Rapid spinning makes you weightless.
Preponderance becomes iteration,
iteration becomes quiet.

Quiet like barren,
quiet like cataracts,
quiet like something you slip into
your pocket and never let out.

I have glowed as much as I could,
in green and other light.
There was nothing left to do but scream.

Now you're waiting for me again,
past the frames holding canvasses
like gums hold teeth.
I'm on my way.

On "A Change in the Water Table" by Kay Sage

Overseas, the churches felt too big and
tubular, windows and arches in one
big swoop. Classmates found them
marvelous, but you were grateful
for the familiar marching orders
—standing, sitting, kneeling—
so you would know when the end
was nearing and you could go to fresher air.

Hotel carpet collects dust, no
matter the housekeepers' efforts.
How strange and stomach-achy,
to work nights in passing-through places.
You hoped their own beds were filled
with their lovers' clean laundry
like warm, friendly animals.

In an animal shelter, the bathroom
had two stalls, and after you washed,
you and another girl went to dry
your hands. You could see the towels
rolled up like tongues inside,
but no matter how much you waved,
the red light wouldn't go. Maybe
we're ghosts, you said, and
you both giggled, but you looked
over your shoulder to check the mirror,
just in case.

You lived in trailer parks, most
of your childhood, learning late metal
chains are meant for swings, and
cinder blocks are immutable. Your
mom worked diners while you shoplifted
sodas in a nearby strip-mall.

And in museums, you wished for
a vending machine you could feed
paperclips because no matter how
fully furnished, you knew it was
nothing more than a rest-stop.

Can nothing be born in places like these?
Surely nothing dies. But if you stay too long,
you will feel it in your stomach,
like a change in the water table.
Water far below ground inches closer.
Capillary action overcomes.

The question now gets turned
inside-out like a skinned rabbit—
can *nothing* be born here?

I have painted always on
the wrong side of my canvasses,
muntins spread out and tense
like the outline of a swing,
like empty dog kennels. Put
down or in homes now, who
is to say? In an empty hotel
room, somewhere, in the off-season,
a maid props her sneakers
up and catches a soap, and
I am folded on top of myself like a prayer.

On "Quote, Unquote" by Kay Sage

This is the end of useless light.
A little later,
with no hope of passing,
I willed it: I walked without echo.
You don't have to be luminous.

A tree will dance.
Listen to the wind.
I didn't want to learn how to dance,
now that I have learned life without leaking.
Serviceable and neat, like a housewarming gift.

The shrieks of a maid.
My floor is huge.
It is shaped like a gun.
Even if you misplaced something, it is not irretrievably lost.
Do you know that ache?

This is the hum of infection. Gentle mouths
know nothing of middle corners.
I was holding up the sky.
The other horses screamed.
I can feel my childhood ending. I

am the voyage of a secret spark.
As lidless as I am,
my favorite safe word is you.
If we end up killing each other,
we will set sail in a red smear.

The red place, underwater. Stillness
on our mantelpiece and another
I want to call murder when
a boat, mid-abortion,
we took its skin off.

I think you would eat the suicides' transgressions.
A woman in a wasps' nest made of paper bags.
A riddle set things in motion.
Listen.
Screaming is only screaming once it crosses over.

And a thousand years from now, your house it
is like a tree felled. My intestines had
stifled any urges.
My small ceremony.
I inhale. I yank it out.

This is what stands between you and home,
in the time of wooden ghosts.
I hate seeing you in our bed.
Be still was what I thought.
I stood in the sun until

the holes are contagious,
sea-changed and on the back.
Did the feathers work for floating?
A whale swims differently than a fly
in the lost animal kingdom.

A journey through which there is no passing.
I think it was looking for a tree.
Your doubt too is a gory miracle.
What color was the moon?
I go to that place; I choose it.

And I am the laugh before you sob.
We won't even bother with food;
I have the back of a scalpel,
to take up completely.
I take my leavings slow and leave.

I have just now figured out what I am trying to say.
Now you're waiting for me again.
Can nothing be born here?

On "Questions Going Nowhere" by Kay Sage

I was here I was here
  I was here
    was here I was here I was here I was here I [i am so fucking sick   ]was here I was here I was here I was here
  I was here I was here I was here I was   of thinking
here I was here I was here I was here I was here I was here I was here I was   about h o l / m e s   here I was here
I was here I was here I was here I was here I was here I was here I was   here I was here I was here I was here I was
here I was here I was here I was here I was here   I was here I was here I was here I was here I was here I was here I was here I was
here I was   here I was here I was here I was here I was here I was here I was here I was here I was here   I was here I was here I was here I was here I was here I was here I

was here   I was here I was here I was here I
       was here I was here I was here I was here I was
here I was here I was here I was here I was here I was here I was
      here I was here   I was here I was here I was
here I was here I was here I was here I was here I was here I was
here I was here I was here I was here I was here I was here I was
here I was here I was here I was here I was here I was here I was
here I was here I was here I was here I was here I was here I was
        here I was here I was here [i am so fucking sick
                  this is the language of sick
this is the language of already gone but its all i got do you want to
                       share it with me
                          [][][][][][][] I was here I was here I
was here I was here I was here I was here I was here I was here I
was here I was here I was here I was here I was here I was here I
was here I was here I was here I was here I was here I was here I
was here I was here I was here I was here I was here I was here I
was here I was here I was here I was here I was here I was here I
was here I was here I was here I was here I was here I was here I
was here I was here I was here I was here I was here I was here I
was here I was here I was here I was here I was here I was here I
was here I was here I was here I was here I was here I was here I
was here I was here I was here I was here I was here I was here I
was here I was here I was here I was here I was here I was here I
was here I was here I was here I was here I was here I was here I
was here I was here I was here I was here I was here I was here I
was here I was here I was here I was here I was here I was here I
             was here I was here I was here

On "No Wind, No Birds" by Kay Sage

We drove, an ice-cream truck on the highway,
my cousin and I, at the end of May,
from his uncle's house in Maine
to my parents' in Vermont.
Summer job, seventeen, and nothing
better to do.
That summer, most afternoons,
we drove around, my cousin
and I. We hummed mercilessly
the jingle to torment each other,
and smoked a lot of cigarettes between stops.
It was a good, hazy feeling,
where everything got a little melty.
By August's end, my cousin got
a new car, so we drove back
to Maine separately, him in the
convertible, me in the truck,
sound turned off. Somewhere in
the dark, I got turned around.
On the highway, at night, lost,
there was no wind, no birds,
just me in the ice-cream truck,
weaving like a zipper through the night.
The trees went blurry like they
melted, the trees went vague
like laundry. They were all I could see,
and now, as if at the end of a long summer,
I am still driving. The trees
say *Your move, Kay Sage*. There
are pine needles in my eyes.
There is darkness in our bellies,
and we are terrified.

On "Watching the Clock" by Kay Sage

here clocks are made from cardboard and bone
she is watching the clock she unpins
the gold one from its nail above the kitchen sink
and hums forces circle into square
why shouldn't she take it with her

time and bones are inflatable watch

$$((((((((((()))))))))))$$
$$((((((((((\qquad\qquad))))))))))$$
$$((((((((((()))))))))))$$
.

Be Still: Poems for Kay Sage

Paul Klee said: "A line is a dot that went for a walk." What, then, is a line of poetry?

*

I've felt insecure about my line breaks this whole time. It's fine that I'm telling you this. You've already read the book. It's too late. I am telling you a secret.

*

Telling secrets is a strange thing to do in poetry. Before this, I had written mostly confessional poetry. And it's had odd ramifications. People assume they know you because you are so frank. They don't know you adore yellow and have an impish sense of humor. They don't know that you memorized everything they've ever told you about their grandmother, because you could tell it was important. All they know is the hospital rooms you've talked about, the massive fracture in your tailbone, and that you have difficulty touching people. They will never guess that there are things you will never, ever write about, because you've told strangers so much shit already.

*

In 2017, you publish your first chapbook. You write about the time your mother tried to kill herself and said it was your fault. You write about what it was like to orgasm while being raped. You write about how it hurts so much now to touch anyone. You write about therapy.

*

Everyone talks about writing like it, too is a journey. I don't believe in time, not anymore. We are not dots, but lines, and those lines intersect again and again. Forget Euclid for a moment, we're free!

*

I have never been around corpses: just the moments after and the bags of flesh that sincerely tried but wound up in hospitals instead. I don't think I would make a great mortician. Besides being dreadful at higher learning, I know I'm not gentle enough.

*

In fall of 2018, your publisher invites to Kansas City, Missouri and read to a crowd of strangers and friends. From Dallas, you drive up with your friend and listen to Janelle Monae to keep awake. There are two jammed-packed days of beer and cigarettes, and, of course, poetry.

You joke with your pressmate that you're siblings now and that your publisher is your dad. *Hey,* you say, *Dad, tell me you're proud of me,* while laughing.

*

I have written the summary of Sage's life in endnotes. And that is profoundly sad to me. *Impending,* that is the word for endnotes, and the most appropriate word for her paintings.

*

I am not and never have pretended to be Sage.

*

How many things can you see at once?

*

A line is a dot that went for a walk, so I walked through Sage's life, in my research. Sage is not one of the artists like Dali or Tanguy where you can find dozens of articles on Google or an affordable used book. (When I started this project, Miller's book had not come out.) I could speculate why Sage hasn't risen to the ranks of a household name, but, again, the information of anything having to do with Sage is incredibly sparse. The fact that the other Surrealists did not accept her could not have helped. Being married to Tanguy could not have helped. I don't know why she means so much to me, so I cannot possibly know why the public all-but forgot about her.

*

People have told me I have a strong personality, and I always blithely say *Thank you,* even though I know it's not necessarily a compliment.

*

On the third day, it's your turn. You read a poem about OCD, a poem about being beaten, a poem about a Kay Sage painting and what it's like to not have a face. You end on a poem about not being able to touch.

*

I have tried my best not to write over Sage's life.

*

I am a gingko tree: lines and lines, fanning out.

*

You look up, and the whole room is crying.

Your publisher is leaving the day before you are. He packs up the unsold books into boxes you can get at dollar stores. He hugs you goodbye. He says *I love you, and I'm so proud of you.*

You think of it days later, driving home from shitty office job that fires you the next week. You cry the whole way home.

*

We are a gingko tree.

*

We can be still, together.

Notes on Poems

All paintings are found in this invaluable book: *Kay Sage: Catalogue Raisonne* by Stephen Robeson Miller, et al. (Del Monico Books/Prestel, 2018). Unless noted otherwise, all citations are from that book.

"Gingo Balboa" by Johann Von Wolfgang Goethe, as found in his work *West-ostlicher Diwan,* 1819.

"Monolith" (1937). Sage titled her suicide note "The end of useless light" (translated from French). She died in 1963 by shooting herself in the heart (25). This is not Sage's first painting, but, in my opinion, it is the first Kay Sage painting.

"A Little Later" (1938). Sage met and fell in love with surrealist painter Yves Tanguy in 1939. Her previous marriage was annulled. The next year, World War II broke out, and Sage left Paris. She arranged for her fellow surrealists to follow. In 1955, Tanguy died suddenly of a cerebral hemorrhage. Sage attempted suicide in 1959 by overdosing on barbiturates (18, 22, 23).

"I Walk Without Echo" (1940). While it is true that Sage had no children, there is no reason to assume she had any desire to or any desire not to. The poem, then, is *gingo bilboba.* The penultimate stanza is borrowed from the title of another Sage painting "Red is Not a Bright Color in the Dark" (1958), whereabouts unknown.

"Danger, Construction Ahead" (1940). From Miller: "From late 1940, and into 1941, [Sage] assisted in helping a number of European artists and intellectuals escape from Europe and resettle in New York. She sought the assistance of her cousin, photographer and sculptor David Hare (1917–1992) who was married to the daughter of President Roosevelt's Secretary of Immigration" (19).

"Pour Yves" (1940). This is the smallest Sage painting, at 7¼ x 6 ¼ inches. Sage and Tanguy were married that year. There has been some speculation as to the nature of their marriage. The TheArtStory.Com article, for example, describes it this way: "Her relationship with Tanguy however was very strong. The two were inseparable, they shared a studio, accompanied each other everywhere, and they communicated in French. Despite such intense togetherness, friends described the marriage as 'strange' and 'uneasy'." But who are we to say what marriages are strange? Are they not small miracles? A thing that is and is not real?

"I Have No Shadow" (1940). Sage's parents separated in 1911, and she lived mostly with her mother who traveled around Europe, chiefly Rome (12).

"A Finger on the Drum" (1940). In 1938, at a salon, Surrealism founder Breton remarked "Kay Sage—man or woman? I didn't know . . . I just knew the paintings were very good" (The Art Story). Despite admiring her work, Breton rejected Sage as a member, likely for being too moneyed and haughty (Miller 12).

"Margin of Silence" (1942). In 1925, Sage married Ranieri di San Faustino, an Italian prince. In 1934, Sage separated from Faustino to pursue a career in art (Miller 15, 17). According to The Art Story article, Sage felt encumbered by the expectations and duties that go along with being married to the elite. In 1959, Sage attempted suicide by barbiturate overdose in her home, where she was found by a maid (The Art Story).

"The Fourteen Daggers" (1942). Miller notes this painting caught the eye of Andre Breton, who used it in his only American exhibition (146).

"Shivering Mountain" (1943). Passages quoted from "Happy Birthday, Johnny" by Annie Clark (St. Vincent). *Masseduction,* Lorna Vista Recordings, 2017. CD.

"Journey to Go" (1943). During her marriage to Faustino, Sage felt unable to paint and that being an artist in her marriage was impossible (15).

"The Giants Dance" (1944). Golden Shovel is a quote from "Summertime Sadness" by Lana Del Rey. *Born to Die,* Interscope Records, 2012. CD.

"Midnight Street" (1944). Miller notes: "The title, subject matter, and nocturnal setting of *Midnight Street* relate directly to a poltergeist experience [Sage] had had in Rome years earlier" (176).

"In the Third Sleep" (1944). In *Catalogue Raisonne,* begins with an essay by Mary Ann Caws, "Kay Sage: Passing Through". Caws notes that in July of 1948, Sage was to have lunch with surrealist painter Ashile Gorky on the day he hung himself, and she was concerned when he called her about having to cancel well after they dined. In 1962, surrealist painter, neighbor, and friend Kurt Seligmann tripped on ice and accidentally shot himself. Tanguy had given him the riffle. Sage was convinced it was suicide. The gun she used a year later was also bought by Tanguy (41–42).

"On the First of March, Crows Begin to Search" (1947). In 1955, Tanguy died suddenly of a cerebral hemorrhage.

"Unicorns Came Down to the Sea" (1948). Sage was beginning to go blind from cataracts before she died by suicide. Oedipus, of course, was blind, from stabbing himself with hairpins after he found out he inadvertently slept with his mother. Before that, he freed the city of Thebes from a riddling sphynx. In the myth of the

Fisher King, the King has a thigh wound and guards the Holy Grail. Unable to walk, he is confined to passing his days in a boat. Percival heals him by asking a question. What that question is varies according to sources. "Pearls for eyes" is an allusion to *The Tempest*. "My mother is a fish" is a chapter from *As I Lay Dying*.

"Tomorrow, Mr. Silber" (1949). Golden Shovel is a quote from "Time Adventure" by Rebecca Sugar, as found in the Cartoon Network show *Adventure Time,* 2018.

"The Outline of Silence" (1950). Anne Carson quote is from her work "Nox," New Directions, 2010. Instructions adapted from a ProFlowers article.

"Men Working" (1951). Lyrics from "Lighthouse" by Patrick Watson, from their album *Adventures in Your Own Backyard,* Secret City Records, 2012, and from "The Geese of Beverly Road" by The National, from their album *Alligator,* Beggars Banquet, 2005.

"Dreamy Cars for Waterbury" (1952). Waterbury, Connecticut is where Sage lived with Tanguy.

"A Bird in the Room" (1955). Per Miller: "The day before Yves Tanguy died of a cerebral hemorrhage in Woodbury, Connecticut, on January 5, 1955, a wild bird got into the room of his and Sage's Town Farm residence. From her years in Italy, Sage knew of a superstition which said that if a wild bird were to get into a house, it meant a fatality would soon occur" (290). After Sage's death by suicide in 1963, her and Tanguy's ashes were scattered by Matisse and Tanguy's sister off the coast of Brittany (24).

"South to Southwesterly Winds Tomorrow" (1957). The story of the missing children is based on the Sodder children disappearance of 1945. The father, George Sodder, believed the five children who stayed up had survived the house fire but were kidnapped by the Sicilian mafia due to his outspoken stance against Mussolini. More information can be found in Karen Abbot's article for The Smithsonian.

"The Answer is No" (1957). Sage's last diary entry reads "I have said all that I have to say. There is nothing left for me to do but scream." In her suicide note, titled "The End of Useless Light," Sage writes: "The first painting I saw by Yves [Tanguy] that I saw, before I knew him, was called I'm Waiting for You. I've come. Now he's waiting for me again—I'm on my way," as found on The Art Story.

"No Wind, No Birds" (1958). The story described is purely fiction. This is the penultimate painting by Sage. As Miller puts it: "As Sage's eyesight had grown worse, she found it increasingly difficult to paint according to her standards, and rather than compromise, she stopped painting altogether" (326). In 1961, she had an exhibition of seventeen object-collages, made from fiber, rocks, eye-glass lenses, and empty bullet cartridges, named *Your Move, Kay Sage* (Miller 24).

"Watching the Clock" (1958). Sage's last painting.

About the Author

Nadia Arioli is the co-founder and editor-in-chief of *Thimble Literary Magazine* and a multi-disciplinary artist. Arioli's poetry has been nominated for Best of the Net three times and can be found in *Cider Press Review, Rust + Moth, San Pedro Review, McNeese Review, Whale Road Review, West Trestle Review, As It Ought To Be, Voicemail Poems, Bombay Literary Magazine,* and other publications. Essays have been nominated for Best of the Net and the Pushcart and can be found in *Hunger Mountain, Heavy Feather Review, Angel Rust,* and elsewhere. Collages and scribblings have been featured as the cover of *Permafrost,* as artist of the month for *Kissing Dynamite* and *Rogue Agent,* and in *Poetry Northwest.*

Arioli has chapbooks with Dancing Girl, Cringe-Worthy Poetry Collective, and Spartan, and a full-length with Luchador Press.

www.ingramcontent.com/pod-product-compliance
Lightning Source LLC
Chambersburg PA
CBHW022135160426
43197CB00009B/1297